70931. Graham Greene Diaries
Vol. II entitled 'A Few Final Journeys'
recording travels to Panama, Nicaragua
Russia + Spain as well as notes relating
to his novel The Captain + The enemy
1986 - 1987. H.23
Cream syntutic binding over boards in
quarter-leather solander case

29,198. Vol. I. 1759-1781 H. J,

Accounts of duels between servants of
East India Company 1759, 1773.

10 Pictures into K DRIVE

About 8 Autographs chopped off the bottom of

38808 B. Autographs mounted on cardboard
descriptions in German at foot. Ernst H. Wei

In October 2002 artist and writer Rachel Lichtenstein became the British Library's first Creative Research Fellow. The Fellowship, which has been sponsored by Pearson since 2004, is part of the Library's learning programme.

Over eighteen months she has run *Meet a Writer* workshops with school groups, teachers and some older learners aiming to inspire ways of researching creatively. Alongside this teaching Rachel has developed her own art project based on the British Library's collections, which has culminated in a photographic installation and this publication.

This project developed from Rachel's own fascination with a variety of original material ranging from the 4th century to the present day. She became intrigued by small sections of text and image, which she then selected to be photographed. At the same time Rachel recorded her research methods and findings in a handwritten journal.

The photographs are a striking group of images that reveal the rich diversity of the Library's collections. They include examples of ephemera, maps, photographs, scrolls, common-place books, personal letters, manuscripts, drawings and poems in a range of languages from many different cultures. These offer a reflection on how the Library contains 'the world's knowledge'. Rachel is sharing these images with a wider audience by creating an interactive art installation in the foyer of the British Library. This artwork will engage visitors through one reader's experience of researching at the Library whilst exposing rarely seen material from the collections.

Bridget McKenzie Head of Learning, The British Library

In 1986 I visited Eduardo Paolozzi's exhibition *Lost Magic Kingdoms and Six Paper Moons* at The Museum of Mankind. The show consisted of several hundred ethnological and anthropological artefacts selected by Paolozzi from the Museum's collections and arranged as assemblages in glass cases. He created a personal vision relating more to his own sculptures and aesthetic sensibilities than to any assumed meanings of the chosen artefacts.

During the making of *Lost Magic Kingdoms* Paolozzi was given a unique opportunity to handle and select artefacts from a rarely seen archive of material. The result was a dynamic exhibition, with strong visual and imaginative impact.

I witnessed the effect that real artefacts can have when handled, during a trip with my children to *Investigate*, the hands-on lab at the Natural History Museum. I watched the excitement on their faces as they picked up a snake's skin and a crocodile's head from hundreds of different specimens and reached their own conclusions with the support of computers, microscopes and measurers. On returning home the imaginative journey continued as they wrote stories about the objects and talked about the experience for weeks.

Their enthusiasm reminded me of my own childhood joy of handling real things. My father worked as an antiques dealer and I often held many old possessions in my hands. A favourite game was to guess who owned each object. It's a powerful tool to the imagination to hold something from a time before you were born and to try to extract its story.

My attraction to objects and their personal histories continues to influence my creative work as an artist and writer. In 1991 I became artist in residence at the Princelet Street Synagogue in London, and had sole access to an undocumented archive of material belonging to the reclusive orthodox scholar David Rodinsky.

He lived in a room above the synagogue for most of his life and disappeared in the 1960s, leaving behind a mystery and a locked room. Through the examination of his personal belongings, and years of historical detective work, I unravelled his life story. The findings are published in *Rodinsky's Room* (Granta, 1999).

I never thought I would have another opportunity to inspect such original material when I came to the Library. In fact this experience is available to anyone lucky enough to have a British Library reader's pass. If you are in possession of this library card, you have direct access to one of the largest collections of material in the world, much of it in its original form.

When I was appointed as the British Library's first Creative Research Fellow I was given the freedom to explore the collections in the broadest sense: without any particular academic criteria in mind. Because of my own my interests I was drawn to the Manuscripts Reading Room with its collection of primary research material. The starting point for my research project was to call up a wide variety of handwritten material and to record my initial impressions in a journal. I looked at hundreds of items, initially selecting them because they looked interesting in the on-line catalogue or because of a personal connection or interest. I viewed musical scores, architectural drawings, journals of voyages, plays and poems. I called up a plan of the siege of the city of Cork in 1690, then a pink velvet case, embroidered with beads and lined with white satin enclosing a love letter. I saw accounts of duels between servants of the East India Company in 1759 and a collection of letters from J.R.R. Tolkien to his grandson. It was not really the content or context of the artefacts that appealed to me but more often their sheer material beauty. I began isolating fragments of text with a viewfinder and enlarging them with a magnifying glass. Seen in such close detail the fragments took on a new

quality, becoming beautiful images in their own right, like paintings. Through this close inspection I became fascinated by details, the marks of time on the pages, spores of mould or sections of text that had rubbed away, like old stone steps in a church. Other minutiae, such as the hairs of a goat woven into the fabric of a page, became the object of my scrutiny. In some books I could see the evidence of human beings behind the text, the marks left by the physical act of writing, such as the greasy fingerprints of a medieval monk. The experience of being in the Reading Room was, for me, magical, spiritual and imaginative, as I tried to reconstruct personal stories from textual shards.

To share the wonder of this experience with a wider audience I arranged for a selection of the items to be photographed to a high specification and enlarged to over fifty times their original size. Twenty-five of these images are the subject of this book and from 19 March – 6 August 2004 they have been arranged as a photographic installation outside the Reader Admissions Office, entitled Add. 17469. The title, like many of the manuscripts displayed, has a variety of meanings and interpretations. I chose these numbers partly because they refer to my own birth date and partly because of the actual item they correspond to in the collections. The manuscript of this reference is a 13th-century set of material, which includes a table of the months according to various nations, a catalogue of the books of the Bible, a life of the Virgin and arguments of the Gospels. This multi-textual document has many resonances with the ideas behind my installation, which in itself is a personal collection of a variety of material from different time periods, cultures and places.

Throughout the duration of the exhibition I have invited curators, scientists, children and members of the public to respond to these images and some of their commentaries have been published here in this book along with my own impressions of the manuscripts when seeing them in their original form in the Reading Rooms. I see every interpretation of the images as new translations of the work, none more significant or necessarily correct than the last. For the librarian the catalogue number will identify the collection the article has originated from. A conservator can sense the importance of the text through the fragility or weight of the paper. A child might respond to the colours and textures of the image. The linguist will understand the content of a foreign text and an artist may lose themselves in the beauty of the blurred ink. Some responses are quotes from texts about the text. Some readers have looked up original material and talked about the smell of the dust trapped between the pages. All of these interpretations are just different ways of reading the same image. We each have a unique point of reference and way of interpreting material, each perspective adding to a rich mosaic of multiple responses. The British Library itself is a place constructed from layer upon layer of different interpretations of our world. A physical place containing 'the world's knowledge', gathered under one roof, with infinite possibilities and infinite directions to expand and grow.

Rachel Lichtenstein

Metro
0x8" pins. dig
£5.50

— providing nude printess position —

DIGITAL IMAGES only. 24 × 2 = 48 image
COMPARE TO 10×8" PRINT OF
DIGITAL + FILM, SAME IMAGE TOTAL OF = 102 ima
THEN DECIDE

54 images

1"
8"
8"
8"
8"
8"
8"
1"

56"

40"

56" ... wooden free structure around plinth, constructed using duratran images

light box

× 1.

86.3/4"

8   8

If true app
10 sessions
× 2 photograph
with camera
10 images in
the ... over res
18 works. Once
amon... afterw
at
... reserve
... day
+ choose wi...
+ photograph
...

Personal diary of the Communist and author Yaroslavsky, written whilst confined in a tsarist prison in Russia, 1909–11. Pencil text with a pressed leaf. (VOL. I, p.39)

——

[illus. previous page]

I found this book under a general search for 'personal diaries'. It's a select manuscript, which means it cannot be left unattended, and suggests that the author is historically significant. When I lifted the heavy diary out of its protective leather box, crumbs of cardboard fell onto my desk from the disintegrating front cover. Inside there were over 300 pages filled with tight pencil script in many different languages, making me think the author had a need to keep his mind active under difficult circumstances. In the centre of the journal are a number of drawings of fellow inmates, a malnourished-looking group of intellectual men, many caught by the artist reading or writing, the sketches now possibly the only surviving record of their existence. As I turned the pages I come across the remnants of a pressed leaf, so fragile I thought at first that it might be a butterfly's wing. Its presence raised many questions for me. Was this a precious object obtained at great risk by the author during a walk in the prison yard? Or a greatly treasured find sandwiched between the pages of a secret journal whose existence threatened his life? Did the leaf remind him of a better life outside the confines of the prison or was this writer a privileged prisoner, allowed to keep a journal and walk freely in a garden where he may have obtained this leaf? R.L.

As the photographer on this project, I found it very interesting viewing items from the British Library's collections from a different perspective. Rachel's project enabled me to go beyond the original meaning and look instead at aspects of design, texture, pattern and form. This new way of examining these works allowed me to view small parts of the whole and to get close to the structure of the material and also to the ageing process on the page.

My choice of image is the decayed leaf, with its vibrant colour, textured veins and shape, as it struck me as being quite poignant, enclosed between the pages of an incarcerated man's diary.

Laurence Pordes Photographer, British Library Photographic Department

Add.71635

Personal diary of the Communist and author Yaroslavsky, written whilst confined in a tsarist prison in Russia, 1909–11. Pencil text with a pressed leaf. (VOL. I, p. 39)

[illus. page 11]

29 Fitzroy Squ...

January

the 1th of your litt...

finger before Easter

next year; a...

I will

get through

on such

forgot to say

to Tuesday. without

was not at "Architec...

he was at mine. If

Apart from maybe a diary, there is no written material more personal than a letter. It's a strange and uncomfortable feeling to sit and read through the private correspondence of people you have never met. There are times when looking at this material feels like prying, although undoubtedly this kind of primary source is invaluable to a deeper understanding of individuals. Personally, I have discovered a new interest in Shaw from reading his letters to Ellen Terry. The hundreds of items in this folio are very intimate, whilst giving a different insight into Shaw's career and rise to fame. They contain decades of intensive and passionate correspondence from him to a lady he obviously admired. Ellen Terry was the most respected English actress of her time and helped Shaw to put on his plays early in his career. She acted in many of his first productions and many letters refer to her roles. Her opinion must have meant a great deal to him, but in this collection Ellen Terry's responses are never heard. What is clear from these letters is his love for her; he writes, 'nobody replaces you in my heart' in a letter dated 1918. Because of the personal nature of this material I decide to photograph a section of a postcard where his words cross over one another in different directions making the text appear coded and therefore remaining private. R.L.

Add.71068

Fragment of postcard from Bernard Shaw to Ellen Terry from a folio of letters, 1892–1928. (F.198, p.55)

———

[*illus. opposite*]

Fragment of post-card from Bernard Shaw to Ellen Terry from a folio of letters, 1892–1928. (F. 198, p. 55)

———

[illus. page 14]

It's the address that does it for me. 'Fitzroy Square'. I wonder whether there's something about the location that drives grown men to despair. It can't be radio waves from the Telecom Tower, because it wasn't built when Bernard Shaw was scribbling his impassioned love-letters to Ellen Terry, a married woman.

I know how this feels. When I lived in that area I was caught up in an impossible love triangle, although the players were less illustrious: Me, Charlotte and Adrian. I worked in the same office as Charlotte, but nobody knew we were living together. Charlotte didn't want this to be common knowledge as she was engaged to Adrian, who was working abroad.

Adrian returned to London having made a fortune in oil and married Charlotte. I quit work and moved to Shoreditch. Unfortunately, to the same street where the poet Thomas Chatterton committed suicide.

I am beginning to suspect that Ellen Terry looked similar to Charlotte, and wonder whether some current inhabitant of Fitzroy Square is going through the same torturous scenario as the one I experienced those miserable years ago.

Anonymous public response

During my research I came across the Hindu word *Dhayana*, which roughly translates as pointed concentration or a type of meditation focused on objects to reveal their true nature. This best describes what I have been trying to do in the Reading Rooms during my fellowship.

Section of a scroll of
a mortuary figure
with a young man;
beside him, three
utensils and a fowl.
By Jogendra
Chitrakar, 1945.
Archer Collection,
watercolour,
Jadupatua style
Hindu imagery.

——

[illus. previous page]

I came across this scroll in the East India Office Select Materials catalogue under a general search for images of Bangladeshi village life. You need to make an appointment in advance to look at this select material, which is viewed in a glass-fronted room off the main Reading Room. Two leather green boxes had been placed on my desk, when I arrived, with a modern book entitled *Indian Popular Painting*, kindly put there by the curator, as it contains a chapter about the folk art in the scroll. On opening the boxes I was surprised to find the scrolls had been sliced into sections and framed in card. I wondered at first if they'd been mounted as 'pictures' to suit Western tastes, but closer inspection revealed the paper was as thin as newsprint and the curator told me that if they'd been kept in their original format they would have been too delicate for public viewing. The surface of the paper is covered in primitive drawings in brightly coloured ink painted with goat hair and porcupine quill brushes by *jadupatuas* or 'magic painters'. These tribal artists earn their livelihood from the scrolls, going from village to village, chanting the stories depicted. The scrolls fascinated me as an amazing example of text and image with multiple functions and many levels of meaning. For the 'magic painters' these were their living and for the precipitants of the scrolls they depicted the stories of their lives. The section I decided to photograph narrates the death of a family member. I focused on a close up image of a fowl with some beautiful handwritten text. Once the 'magic painter' had drawn the bird it had to be given to the painter as payment by the bereaved family. R. L.

This is a fragment of a larger painting. It was created in the Santal region of Bihar (Eastern India) by an artist named Jogendra Chitrakar, in around 1945. This part of the picture shows a bird and part of a Bengali inscription. A British man collected this painting, along with a series of scroll paintings, while he was employed by the British government in India in the mid 1940s. Soon after he collected this group of paintings, India became [an] independent [country]. The information accompanying these pictures was collected by the same British man.

In the 1960s this painting and the scrolls painted by Jogendra Chitrakar became part of the India Office Collections. The scrolls were cut into sections so they could be stored flat instead of in rolls. Such alterations to objects are no longer performed or condoned by conservators and curators. It has recently become popular to reconstruct the original form of such fragmented documents through digital imaging. Considering the history of this picture, and the scrolls it was collected with, I find it ironic that only a small detail of a larger composition is shown here.

Jennifer Howes Curator, India Office Archives

Section of a scroll of a mortuary figure with a young man; beside him, three utensils and a fowl. By Jogendra Chitrakar, 1945. Archer Collection, watercolour, Jadupatua style Hindu imagery.

———

[illus. page 17]

of Ibraim is a large well with
accessible only from the river. —

Vases of all shapes of Alabaster
hes. —   as well as the commones
war
em — or made of Stone, if small,
very coo

osij
ldem
the
the
ins
b

Design for a small table —

During my researches I called up a number of journals. Most were 19th century and recorded travels and observations of foreign places by English men. There is something so particularly British about the pages gathered here from this expedition. The text reveals a detached observation of a very different environment from the author's own. Little personal perspective or experience has been added to the documents but within the collected pages it is never clear if this is a personal diary or notes to be handed over to an employer of some kind. It is clear from reading the papers that Mr Hay visited Egypt repeatedly and took numerous trips to temples where he copied details of hieroglyphics and statues. Near the back of the book is an inventory of treasures including, 'ten scarabs, a gold python, a bronze altar and a black vase'. The destination of these artefacts is never clear. Apart from being a fascinating read, the main reason I am so personally attracted to these papers is because they are so beautiful. Hundreds of fragments of notes, letters, sketches and lists have been painstakingly gathered together and bound into a tactile book of different sized papers of varying weight. The surface of these papers is covered in either pencil drawings or a very distinctive ink script. Where the different layers of paper overlap is the point that I decide to photograph in an attempt to convey my pleasure of looking at and feeling the texture of this remarkable document. **R. L.**

Add.29,859

Overlapping pages from papers relating to Robert Hay's Egyptian expedition, 1835. (VOL. XLVIII, F. 30, p. 16)

———

[illus. opposite]

God
Royal
Goddess
Wife
Father
Mother
Add. 34, 088
EGYPT
1PM
outside
Humanities
1.
Ask Bridgett
Bumped in to someone hadn't seen for 15 yrs today
make sure
Ken has copies
of photo references
to send to lab

I try to interpret the squiggly writing but can't seem to read it. After staring at it for a while I start to recognise some of the words. This changes my whole perspective of the piece. I think this writer has a problem with spelling e.g. 'wile' (while). The pictures make me think this man has found or is looking for something. The map, the word 'river' – all suggest the Nile in Egypt. I imagine a man in khaki with a ridiculous slightly curled moustache. This piece could be part of his diary. This all conjures a scene from Indiana Jones. These are my thoughts.

Aziz Hasan Age eleven years

Add.29,859

Overlapping pages from papers relating to Robert Hay's Egyptian expedition, 1835. (VOL. XLVIII, F. 30, p. 16)

[illus. page 20]

These fragmented images from the collections are parts of broken narratives, waiting for voices to bring them to life.

I'm overwhelmed to have this folder of material in my hands, being a great fan of Rosenberg's, his story forming part of the mythology of Whitechapel, my home and inspiration for over a decade. Isaac Rosenberg was born in 1890 and died at only twenty-seven years old in the trenches of the Somme. He was a gifted visual artist and Jewish war poet. His family emigrated from Russia to England before he was born and he spent most of his short life living in East London. I have sat in the seat he frequently used, upstairs in the Reading Rooms of the Whitechapel Library, and heard the librarians talking about books he desecrated there by writing poems in the margins. He was known to meet in the library with a group of radical Jewish intellectuals known as the 'Whitechapel Boys'. I have met a school teacher who moved to Whitechapel just so he could walk the same streets as Rosenberg once walked and here I am in the British Library looking at a few fragile pieces of paper with poems and notes written in his own hand. The paper is worn and delicate, covered in a mixture of faded ink, old typewriter face, pencil and coded sketches. 'A little dust whispered, a little grey dust' is written on one of these paper fragments. His words move me but it is the back of one of the pages themselves that I choose to photograph; a beautiful cross of different papers glued together by conservationists to support and preserve the letter on the other side. To me the fragility of the paper and the cross, itself a reminder of death, act as a metaphor for his own life which was cut short during the carnage of World War One. The resulting image could take its place on the wall of any contemporary art gallery. R. L.

Isaac Rosenberg poem, 1917, from a collection of drafts, partly in pencil, including some typescript, 1905–1917. (Verso p. 28)

——

[illus. page 24]

Isaac Rosenberg
poem, 1917, from
a collection of
drafts, partly in
pencil, including
some typescript,
1905–1917.
(Verso p. 28)

——

[illus. page 24]

If the American artist Robert Rauschenberg had ever painted the St George Cross I imagine that it would have looked like this. The cross is a loaded and potentially threatening symbol; this image contains a quiet optimism.

In 1951 Rauschenberg created a series of 'White Paintings'. He was experimenting with degrees of painterly abstraction, reducing paint to its essential qualities in order to represent pure experience. The paintings were both 'built up' and 'stripped back', neither one nor the other, in limbo. Square and rectangular canvases were layered with ordinary white house paint to create a smooth surface. The meaning of the canvas was then created in situ. Patterns, lights and shadows danced across their surface, reflecting the dynamics of the real life and real time of the exhibition environment.

This image looks like a 'white painted' St George flag, unsure of itself, both 'built up' on its reputation and 'stripped back' to a ghost of itself, vulnerable, in limbo. There is quietness here, jingoism shut down, made to think. It is forced to become a reflexive surface that cannot help but offer itself to capture an infinite range of experiences.

Dr Joanne Lacey Lecturer in Media Studies, British Library Reader

Papyrus 447

Single piece in glass case. Document of doubtful nature owing the to extent of its mutilations. Latin, 4th century.

——

[illus. previous page]

Is there another place in the country where you are able to hold something from the 4th century in your hands? I called up this piece of ancient papyrus purely for the experience of doing this. I waited for over an hour for the green light to come on at my desk before going to collect it. A wooden tray lined with padded white leather was handed over to me and resting inside was an exquisitely fragile and decaying piece of papyrus sandwiched between two sheets of glass, bound together with red leather straps. I carefully took the tray back to my desk and bent down to inspect it in detail until I became lost in the patterns on the surface. It seems incredible that such a damaged fragment has survived all this time; just looking at it makes my heart beat faster. The right hand side of the single piece of woven paper has deteriorated so much I cannot see a single pencil mark upon it. But I can see the strands of the fibres in the reeds it was made from, and the many holes now present in the parchment look like a language all of their own, an inverted sort of Braille. I try to copy the only readable text on the top left of the page.

To be so close to an artefact like this is an exhilarating experience. I may not understand the meaning of what I am looking at but I do appreciate the awesome opportunity I have been given by sitting in front of this material. R. L.

Single piece in glass case. Document of doubtful nature owing the to extent of its mutilations. Latin, 4th century.

———

[illus. page 27]

I see this as a textile, both a tile of text and a woven thing. This piece of papyrus is woven from threads of reed. A text is woven from threads of meaning. The Latin verb *texere* means 'to weave', giving us textile, tissue and text. This relates to the Greek word *tekhne* for 'skill', giving us technology. Texts rely on technology, whether that is the skill of weaving reeds or hypertext. The weaving of texts follows a thread from sound to word to image. This thread must have started with the tangled voices and practices of 'the houses' where scribes and officials agreed what must be recorded and what the signs would mean. The Egyptian word *papyri*, giving us paper, means 'from the house' or 'from the bureaucracy of the kings'. Many of the billions of paper sheets archived in the Library are 'from the houses' of churches, kings, trading companies and universities. Others, especially those from modern times as paper has become more affordable, are 'from the house' in that a private individual has written for herself. Now, we prefer to read writing that is 'from the house' in this domestic way as it speaks directly to us, and we even prefer our bureaucratic or public writing to have a personal voice. Rachel is reading these old texts entirely framed by that modern preference, immersing herself in the history of the texts not through historical method but by listening out for the originating voices and feeling their craft with her hands.

Bridget McKenzie Head of Learning, The British Library

Negative imprint
of a pen-and-ink
sketch of a
Transylvanian
Gypsy by Joseph
Pennell, 1891.
(Verso p.40)

——

[illus. previous page]

On seeing the title of this book I was too curious not to call it up. It sounded so
exotic, a 19th-century collection entitled *Drawings of Transylvanian Gypsies
on the Russian frontier*. The real thing did not disappoint. The book is as thick as
a telephone directory, filled with over one hundred technically skilful drawings,
pen-and-ink sketches and paintings of gypsies and gypsy life mounted onto card.
Underneath each image is a small description by the artist, for example 'gypsy
women selling clothes', 'a cello player in the market place'. The thickness of the
card makes the pages heavy and hard to turn, increasing the vulnerability of
the document, which seems to lose a little bit of itself every time you turn a
page due to the brittle nature of the cardboard mounts. Whilst the drawings
are beautiful, seeing them made me want to look at photographs of the same
subject. It is unlikely that any exist. Photography was still in its early stages in
the 1890s and it may not have been possible to take the amount of equipment
needed to the remote places featured in these images. The gypsies themselves
might also have been unwilling to have their image captured by camera.
The realisation that these few original drawings may be the only record of this
particular community's way of life at this time makes the book priceless.

On page 41 is a gouache monochrome painting of three gypsies standing
in a field entitled *Gypsy Land: an arrangement in black and white*. The pressure of
the heavy book having been closed for over a hundred years has caused an imprint
of the painting to appear on the opposite page, like the negative of a photograph.
The paint's grease has been embedded into the paper, leaving a forensic residue,
which looks like an X-ray, a ghostly impression of a lost community. R.L.

A book is not just an object that you hold in your hands. It is a multi-dimensional space full of ideas from many sources, authors and time periods.

When I was a girl, grown ups asked, "What would you like to be when you grow up?" I said, "I want to be a guy spy." "What's a guy spy?" they said. They didn't know I was dyslexic. I meant a gypsy and I wanted to live in a moving home. My Mother taught traveller children. If you called them gypsies, that was rude. She had a mobile classroom with a shower inside. Sometimes my clothes went missing, and books and toys and my Mother said that the traveller children needed them because they didn't have much. But they had a moving home. I wanted a moving home.

Transylvania: a place in Romania across the woods
Transcendental: going beyond human knowledge and into a spiritual area
Transcribe: put thoughts into written form
Transfer: move from one place to another
Transfigure: transformed into something more beautiful or spiritual
Transform: marked change in appearance, form or nature
Transgress: go beyond the limits
Transient: staying for a short time
Transit: the carrying of people and things from one place to another
Translucent: allowing light to pass through
Transmigration: the passing of a person's soul after their death into another body
Transmit: allow to pass through a medium
Transmogrify: humorous change into something else in a magical manner
Transmute: change in form, nature or substance
Transplant: transfer to another place or situation
Transpose: cause to change places with each other/write or play in a different key

Vanessa Lee   British Library Reader

Add.63141

Photograph by
Takayoshi Yoda
for Mainichi
Newspapers,
Tokyo, no date.
Blakeney Collection
(VOL. II, F. 23, p. 17)
———

[*illus. previous page*]

Many of the images I've selected are from documents about travel of some kind. Sometimes they record physical voyages, other times they detail personal and imaginative journeys. The Blakeney collection does all of this. It consists of hundreds of matchbox-sized, loose black-and-white images, along with a private collection of photographs and newspaper cuttings encapsulated in melinex folders and bound within a large box. The first thing you see when opening the box is a handwritten note on a torn piece of paper in blue ink, (written by an unknown hand, although it looks contemporary), saying 'Hudson, Rev. Charles (1825–1865) Vicar of Shillington Lancs 1859–65. Best amateur Alpinist of his time, killed in a fall descending the Mattahorn.' How this relates to the images I do not know, as the back of the first photograph is dated 1947. You are left reconstructing stories from such enticing textual shards. The small black-and-white photographs are an eclectic mix, documenting worldwide travel by Blakeney and his wife, including pictures of African tribesmen, elephants, Victoria Falls and rare glimpses into Tibetan life in the 1940s. Half of the book is filled with these personal snapshots. The other half contains photos of mountain climbs and climbers, from Victorian times to the 1950s, as well as maps and plans for mountain ascents and a newspaper cutting of an astronaut, along with other bits of ephemera. The collection has been gathered together from different materials and sources, from various time periods, mediums and places. Because of this the material nature and aesthetic look of the book is varied, tactile and in my opinion exquisitely beautiful. I selected a plan for a mountain ascent to photograph, detailing a section of a black-and-white image covered in tracing paper and thick red wax pencil. R. L.

Written marks over an image of a landscape – a reminder of how we make sense of the world, how we orient ourselves within space. It is as if the marks are a record of a journey over the hills, mapping, trying to reduce the earth to something comprehensible, but always revealing a personal presence; as personal as a footprint on a mountain or a line drawn over an image.

Anonymous public response

This looks like a racing car going up a mountain really fast. I like to climb huge mountains. Red lines show where the car has been and how fast.

Michael Age five years, from Newcastle

Add.63141

Photograph by
Takayoshi Yoda
for Mainichi
Newspapers,
Tokyo, no date.
Blakeney Collection
(VOL. II, F.23, p.17)

[illus. page 35]

This is a select manuscript that arrived on my desk boxed in green leather with a gold trim. I carefully opened it up and extracted the travelogue. A librarian wandered past at regular intervals, throwing me a backward glance every now and then. Inside the front cover '£7500' is written in pencil and I wondered if the diary has been bought by the Library in an auction or donated. Every page of the book is covered in shaky handwriting from a thick-nibbed blue ink pen. The writing is orderly but almost impossible to decipher as if it has been deliberately written in code like Leonardo da Vinci's notebooks. I struggled to read it for over an hour, managing only to pick out single words like 'heat', 'drinking', 'Havana', 'prostitutes' and 'bed', the words creating an aura of violence and danger in a distant, exotic location. I wondered if his writing is a reflection of inner turmoil or whether he learnt how to write like this during his time as an MI6 spy. Maybe it's a coded form of personal shorthand to protect his writing from someone like me, trying to read his private, unpublished thoughts. It's something I often think about whilst researching in the manuscripts room. Is it morally right for any reader to be able to leaf through the private journals and diaries of those long dead, who almost certainly never intended for these documents to be made public property? Out of a desire to protect his privacy I have decided to photograph a tiny section of his nearly illegible handwriting which transforms into a series of painterly marks. R. L.

Add. 70931

Detail from Graham Greene's diary entitled *A Few Final Journeys*, recording travels to Panama, Nicaragua, Russia and Spain, and including notes relating to his novel *The Captain and the Enemy*, 1986–1987. (VOL. II, F. 23, p. 17)

[illus. opposite]

Every page feels like a layer of earth waiting to be excavated.

'restaurant …hideous …impossible …wine' Graham Greene's words are scratched out as if a spider had crawled from a pot of royal blue ink and made its cantankerous way across the page. This graphic is taken from one of two notebooks kept by the author and lugubriously entitled *A Few Final Journeys*. Greene was famously covert, evasive, mysterious in his movements. His journal is all the more valuable, then, for allowing us an insight into a punishing itinerary (is that the word 'tired' we can discern?) made during the last five years of his life as he travels through Panama, Nicaragua, Russia and Spain. An extraordinary itinerary in which, for example, a meeting with Panama's military leader, Manuel Noriega, is given no more weight than a bad meal in a restaurant.

Chris Fletcher Curator of Manuscripts, The British Library

An author's handwriting. Always completely illegible. Faced with a piece of text, my editor's instincts jump into action. What is he trying to say? Is the punctuation correct? I soon realise this is a futile task as the writing is hard to read. The word 'impossible' takes centre stage, and below: is that 'two of wine'?

I stop focusing on the words and start to enjoy it as an image. I turn it sideways and it becomes unusual, vertical script, unrecognisable as English. Greene's pen seems to splutter on the page, filling up the holes in an 'o' or a 'p'. We could typeset this text and all would be legible, but once set, any misreading might go down in history as fact: 'two of wine' or 'two of mine'? As a fragment we can ignore the words and enjoy his incomprehensible design, and as a handwritten diary we cannot be sure what it says.

Georgina Difford Publishing, The British Library

Add.70931

Detail from
Graham Greene's
diary entitled
A Few Final Journeys,
recording travels to
Panama, Nicaragua,
Russia and Spain,
and including notes
relating to his novel
*The Captain and the
Enemy*, 1986–1987.
(VOL. II, F.23, p.17)

———

[*illus. page 38*]

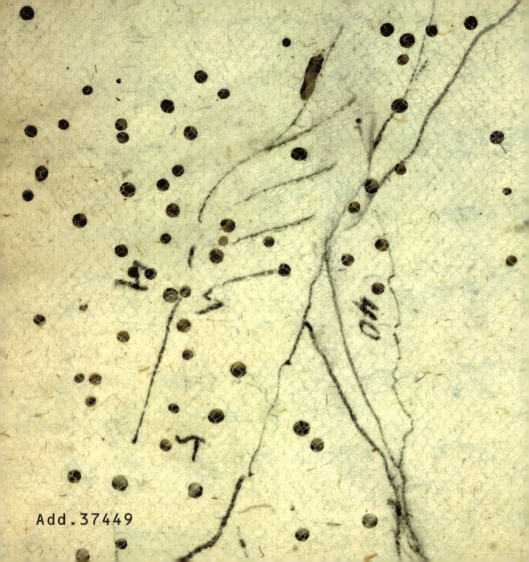

Add.37449

Another journal from Egypt with a very different feel to the last, having been written by a man from Armenia, employed in the Egyptian service, mainly concerning archaeological excavations. His journals include records and sketches of these excavations and a number of personal letters, drawings, maps and papers. I spent a considerable amount of time looking through a number of Hékékyan's journals. They are just such beautiful objects. In my opinion their beauty is due to a number of different factors – much credit must go the author and the style and quality of his handiwork, but the holes left by bookworms add mystery and texture to the pages. They've eaten their way through large sections of these journals, creating worm holes that literally carve out new paths in the text. Their destruction has deleted parts of the script whilst adding a new, dimensional feel to the document. Intervention by the paper conservator has stopped the process of time and decay destroying these documents entirely, but the majority of the journals have already been badly eaten away. My interest in this map is purely aesthetic. Turned on its side it looks like a figure drawing; the worm holes add another layer to the image and the texture of the map is rough due to the fine film of mesh netting that is holding the remnants of the page together. Seeing this image and the obvious craft involved in conserving such a page inspired me to visit the Conservation Department to see how this was done. R.L.

Add.37449

Detail of a map from the journal and private correspondence of Joseph Hékékyan Bey, an Armenian in the Egyptian service, 1841–1844. (VOL.II, p.337)

———

[illus. opposite]

'A series of marks to
be deciphered.'

I had planned to respond to this fragment purely as an image, as I might respond to a painting or photograph on the wall of a gallery. To look for meaning or inherent interest in Add.37449 proved impossible. An image can never have an entirely separate life from its context, a somehow 'pure' existence and I found my concentration straying quickly.

Firstly I ask myself what I already knew of the image. I already know too much, and too little. I know that it isn't a work of art in its entirety. It is a fragment connected to Rachel Lichtenstein's work at the British Library. That is where my knowledge ends. It is frustrating. The image may have been created deliberately, may be a small part of an illustration or a painting. Then again, the fine lines and splatters could be accidental, a by-product of age or misuse, the image nothing but stains created by mould.

The 'title' begins to take on huge significance. What does Add.37449 mean? It suggests a cataloguing system, perhaps the image could be traced with this number. I could go to the Library and find out where it comes from, give Add.37449 context and meaning. What will I find? Perhaps the image is an extreme enlargement from a book, and a huge, very old leather bound and precious tome will be brought up ceremoniously from deep within the Archives, covered with centuries of dust.

I realise I have left the fragment behind completely and am beginning to fantasise. I want the bigger picture.

Sue Jones Curator of contemporary art

Detail of a map from the journal and private correspondence of Joseph Hékékyan Bey, an Armenian in the Egyptian service, 1841–1844. (VOL. II, p. 337)

[illus. page 42]

2 boxes Self fitting Cand[?]

A bunch of Parsley =

¼ lb Chocolate Menier[?]

½ lb Sultanas .

½ lb Raisins .

¼ lb. Glacé Cherries

Whilst leafing through Bernard Shaw's impassioned correspondence to Ellen Terry I was surprised to come across a shopping list. The list is obviously written in a different hand to the other letters and I cannot imagine Shaw would send a note to Terry on the back of an old shopping list. Everything about the letters he writes to her is considered, each being produced on good quality paper written in ink pen with a careful hand. The shopping list looks as if it has been written at great speed, the handwriting is sloppy, the ink smeared, the words crossed out.

By reading through Shaw's forty years' worth of letters to Ellen Terry I learnt that much to Shaw's distress she married someone else. I imagine her husband was not delighted about the lengthy letters Shaw continued to send to his wife after their wedding. This is not discussed directly in the letters but the shopping list tells another story. I suspect it was written by Terry's jealous husband as, underneath the list, are the sarcastic words:

'Oh no, a letter from George Bernard Shaw on the other side, what a pity! Oh the sugar and the bacon, the servants and the drains!' R.L.

Shopping list on the back of a letter from Bernard Shaw, 1898. From a folio of letters from Bernard Shaw to Ellen Terry, 1892–1928. (F.198, p.187)

———

[illus. opposite]

47

Shopping list on
the back of a letter
from Bernard Shaw,
1898. From a folio
of letters from
Bernard Shaw
to Ellen Terry,
1892–1928.
(F.198, p.187)

[illus. page 46]

I think this is a
recipe for a cake.
by David H.L.
age five

48

A sculpture exists in its relationship to the viewer. There is a need to participate with it. I want this book to have that same quality.

Archeology doesn't
necessarily tell any
truths. Its a series
of fictions like
any narration.

...en close + put new image in

I was thinking that you might find interesting early material if you look in the printed catalogues to 19...
...ding "London", and at the end there is a big section called "Appendix" which is subdivided into history...
...used to enter all sorts of material about London as an early attempt at a subject index. The real Sub...
...'t start until 1880, and the published volumes are in hum 1.

אָנָּא אֵל נָא רְפָא נָא לָהּ

Ana El na r'fah na li.

At certain point became less conscio...
of the journal being public, fr...
rather took my own advice, ...
to children. O.k. to make
mistakes, to write in diff. la...
Yisrael Lode, to be messy

Bethsimuth

DEAD SEA

Add.29859

Most of the manuscripts I've selected have no particular personal significance to me but drawn into the back pages of Hay's private journal I find a map that marks out a route I have travelled many times. In the mid-nineties I spent over a year living in a small place about a mile away from the Dead Sea called Arad; a 1950s Israeli pioneer town on the edge of the Negev desert. When this map was drawn, Arad and most of the other places I got to know in that area did not exist.

The author of the map has not attempted to describe the area in its totality but rather to detail his own journey from one place to another, remapping a place from his own reference points. This is something I am able to do as I look at his map, as I know many of the places he passes on route from Jerusalem to Jericho extremely well. It's a fascinating project, to compare a 19th-century map of a place you know with your own mental map. Few places in the world have probably changed as much in this time period as this former part of Palestine. When the map was drawn, the area was so uninhabited that there were few towns or cities to describe. Instead, the artist chooses to portray landmarks on the route by their physical descriptions, such as 'deep glen, ruinous castle, clump of rocks and ruined bridge'. The Bedouins you meet in the desert today would do the same thing. The only places that are constant on Hay's map and which are also contemporary are Jerusalem, Jericho, Nazareth and the Dead Sea. I select a fragment of the map to photograph showing the Dead Sea; the resulting image looks like a bleeding wound. R.L.

Detail of map showing journey from Jerusalem to Jericho, from papers relating to Robert Hay's Egyptian expedition, 1835. (F.43)

———

[illus. opposite]

Detail of map show-
ing journey from
Jerusalem to Jericho,
from papers relating
to Robert Hay's
Egyptian expedition,
1835. (F.43)

———

[illus. page 50]

A fine abstract of a journey I once took on a bus with a maniac driver over thirty years ago. Jericho was the most remote spot on earth to which I had ever been. The colour of the sea is presumably at least ten times older.

John Irish Reader

...ου ἐγκαίρως ἐδεξάμην, ἀλλὰ δυσ...

...κουρῶ καὶ οὐ δύναμαι ἐξελθεῖν τ...

...θυμῶν βίαν ἐξελθεῖν. Διὸ, δέομα...

...έροις τὸ ἄχρις ἡμέρας μεταφρασθ...

...οια αὐτοῦ ἐρμηνεύσομεν ὕστερο...

...ηδος μοὶ γράφει ἐκ Λονδίνου, ...

...η μήπω κοινοποιήσεως τοῦ ἔργου...

...ν ἐφημερίδων βλάπτει με τὰ...

...με, ἵνα ἐπιταχύνω τὴν διάδοσιν...

...οὐδὲν πλέον. ἔρρωσο.

Section of a letter
from Simonides to
John E. Hodgkin.
Greek, 1860–1865.
(VOL. I, F.388, p.113)
———

[illus. previous page]

This folio is packed full of numerous handwritten letters in Greek and English, beautifully presented in a large leather book. Most of the letters in the front half of the book are from Simonides to Hodgkin and the majority are written in Greek. The latter half is filled with correspondence concerning Simonides, including legal battles and an announcement of his death: 'Poor fellow, he died in great poverty from leprosy. May God have mercy on his soul.' (From a letter dated 1865). As I examine these fragile documents I cannot help but mourn the near passing of the handwritten letter. The weight and different textures of the many papers are a joy to hold. These letters obviously meant a great deal to their owner to have been kept so carefully for so long. I know that some of my most precious belongings are personal letters. So much can be told about the relationship between two people by the paper chosen to write on, the quality of the envelope it's sent in, the superiority of the pen and ink used, if the letter is scented or not. The beautiful handwritten script in this book is in a language I do not understand but I see it as an art form in its own right. I choose to photograph a section of a page where pink Greek script has slightly blurred. I would gladly hang the enlarged image on my wall in the place of an abstract painting. R.L.

I have no knowledge of the meaning of the words, their age or context, or the identities of the writer or recipient. I have resisted searching for meaning, relying instead on my own immediate, unlearned reading.

In fact, not knowing allows me to look at the pale of the parchment, the deep pink of the ink, the watery shadow of the text as what I imagine them to be – words of love.

The haste of the hand suggests to me a flow of feeling, the hue of the ink, passion. It signifies what it does because of my mood, my will to believe and the time of the year and where I am when I have seen it – in the early, hopeful romance of spring.

If I follow the gentle riot of my imagination, how much right do I really have to know what these words mean? It feels like an intrusion into the love I have so wilfully imagined, to experience these feelings alongside them.

I wish I had been lucky enough to receive the shadowed excitement of this letter, the determination, the pink sky of morning that is part of not being able to sleep.

Fiona Perrin Writer

Add. 42502 A

Section of a letter from Simonides to John E. Hodgkin. Greek, 1860–1865. (VOL. I, F. 388, p. 113)

[illus. page 53]

[Collected Works,
1937, p. 232.]

Delights!
All pleasures fly!
O clinging lights
And wavering glory
Adieu you sigh,
Half told your story
To you we die

Through the magnifying glass, the marks on the paper take on their own landscape.

The treasures in the British Library are not just first editions and jewel-encrusted, priceless bibles. They include tiny scraps of paper, torn fragments of letters and other fragile bits of ephemera, lovingly restored and protected for future generations. It's a miracle that some of it has survived and this torn envelope with a poem verse by Isaac Rosenberg is no exception. Rosenberg died very young and little of his original material exists. He was notoriously forgetful and often failed to remember to address letters he wrote, making an envelope with his writing on it a rare artefact.

Decades after the author's untimely death, I call up a folio of Rosenberg's letters from the holdings of the British Library and find this envelope. Touching it sparks a number of possible scenarios, was it sent to a beloved from the trenches of the Somme? Did Rosenberg write it on the back of an envelope that came to hand whilst sitting in a coffee shop in Whitechapel? Was it found in the inside pocket of his uniform when his dead body was searched? This stained envelope covered in pencil text, containing the verse of a poem from one of Britain's most revered First World War poets, is a beautiful object in its own right. I hope this project will inspire others to go to the Reading Rooms and call up these remarkable artefacts for themselves. R.L.

Add.48210

Isaac Rosenberg poem fragment on back of envelope *All Pleasures Fly*, 1917, from a collection of drafts, partly in pencil, including some typescript, 1905–1917. (F.33)

[illus. page 56]

Isaac Rosenberg poem fragment on back of envelope *All Pleasures Fly*, 1917, from a collection of drafts, partly in pencil, including some typescript, 1905–1917. (F.33)

———

[illus. page 56]

The envelope is itself a fragment, torn at the bottom and top, the area of writing – which crosses the glued joins of the paper – somehow unscathed. The words may have been written in a moment of calm in the trenches, in 1914 before he joined up, in a shard of peace, in a passing moment of memory.

The single word, first line, or title possibly, is crossed out (it was the word 'Delights!'), the change of 'die' to 'fly'. The first word of the final line reads as 'To': and yet it nags at me, the 'T' resembling an 'F', and I wonder if Rosenberg was in half a mind to write 'For' rather than 'To'. 'For you we die': but then thought better of it – 'To you' is more the meaning he had in mind, dictated by the terror and stupidity of the war. And then his words are of dearthing pleasures, clinging lights, wavering glory, un-Georgian poetry in a sort of Georgian language. Early postcolonial: he came from Yiddish and Hebrew, and his own rich and beautiful English shows this rooted and asylumed gift.

Rosenberg went to war from economic necessity, to provide for his family, and died a few days short of war's end. Sometimes I wonder what he might have written after the war, what he might have said, what he might have done, though it doesn't much help to so wonder. A hundred years ago he would have been walking these Whitechapel streets I know so well. I still see him walking sometimes, on his way from Dempsey Street to the Library, on his way from Leftwich and Rodker to his home.

Stephen Watts British Library Reader, Poet

Papers relating to
the War of Candia,
reporting Venetian
military actions in
Crete. Italian, 1669
(from May 22 1667
to 14 April 1669).

———

[illus. previous page]

I decide to look at this book out of sheer curiosity. Inside the beautifully made leather binding are hundreds of pages filled with delicate handmade paper covered in fine ink lettering written in Italian. Towards the end of the book the handwriting style seems to change, so it seems probable there were two authors. The paper becomes thinner in the last fifty pages of the book and suddenly you can clearly see the silhouette of the writing on the back of the page like veins in a leaf. I choose the central section to photograph and decide to go in really close and focus on two words. The first is written in fading sepia ink and you can imagine that this was the point when the writer of the text dipped his quill into the ink pot, since the next word is dark and fat and the edges of the letter have bled slightly into the page because of the substantial amount of ink used. I examine the letters closely using a magnifying glass and as I get closer I manage to snort a large quantity of fine dust from the book's surface which makes me sneeze violently. This is of course an unforgivable and highly dangerous thing to do near to an irreplaceable 17th-century manuscript. The curator sitting on the raised desk in the centre of the Reading Room eyes me suspiciously. 'Allergies', I mouth, 'sorry'. His face remains stony and I notice him peering at me constantly over his glasses throughout the morning. R.L.

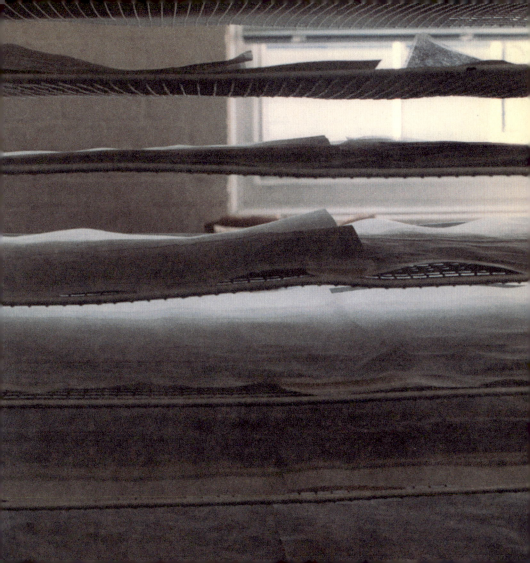

Papers relating to
the War of Candia,
reporting Venetian
military actions in
Crete. Italian, 1669
(from May 22 1667
to 14 April 1669).

———

[illus. page 59]

For me there is a connection between the idea of the ink fading out as the pen moves across the page, and the idea of Venice's position as a major international power fading away during the seventeenth century – we don't see clearly the entire process of the ink fading so much as see that it has happened. And as the ink runs out the flourishes within the letters become more, more what? More decorative? More carefree? More desperate? More affirmative of the writer's need to leave an individual mark? The ghost of the script on the other side of the page acts as a visual reminder that the text is about striving and conflict.

Julian Walker Artist

Royal.14.C.I

———

[illus. previous page]

As I open this illuminated manuscript a pungent animal smell almost causes me to retch. I later discover the pages are made of vellum, a material made from fine sheets of calf bellies. It has a waxy texture and feels smooth, supple and strong with surprisingly few irregularities on the surface. The colours of the inks are so bright it's hard to believe the book is over half a millennium old. I carefully rest the document on a black cushion shaped like an open book, which is how fragile material and ancient manuscripts are viewed here. The pages are gently held open with a 'snake', a kind of cotton string of beads that is heavy enough to hold them back without damaging them. When I do turn the pages they sound like rustling leaves. If you cannot interpret the text there are few visible indications as to the age of this document, apart from the corners of the pages, which are as thin as greaseproof paper from the pressure of many hands turning them over time. In the centre of the book is a double page that appears to have been accidentally left blank. Faint pencil lines have been drawn in readiness for a text that never materialised. Instead a small trace of the author has been left upon the page, a personal DNA signature in the form of two greasy fingerprints possibly deposited there by the monk who spent most of his life writing this text. The thumbprints and pencil lines on vellum, taken out of context and presented in the form of a magnified digital image, look fresh and contemporary, reminding me of one of Eva Hesse's drawings. R.L.

By intervening with technology, the magnified image allows for a more detailed examination of the selected fragments just like in a forensic investigation, the process adding a new layer to the original meaning of each page, which is now open to multiple interpretations.

Finger prints on vellum capture a moment in time, a record of a touch which is incidental rather than planned but however remains a permanent record. Life is like that, we touch others and the world around us in transit all the time and in doing so we leave behind a trace, a personal signature.

Carol Foulds

Historical works of William Rishanger, Martinus Polonus & Geoffrey Monmouth. Pencil with finger-prints on vellum. Latin, 14th century. (F.7)

———

[illus. page 63]

καρτερι-

Σιμωνίδου, ὁ δέ

καρτερικῶς ἔχει

μόνος

ἵσταται μάχεται

πρὸς ὅλους

Every detail of text that I have had photographed has been chosen with the same consideration – as if I were an art curator selecting images for an exhibition. This figurative sample of Greek text, shaped in a geometric pattern, has a strong visual impact in its design and a resonance in its meaning for this project as a whole. The majority of the photographs are images of text that become independent pictures in their own right, each forming a part of a visually exciting art installation shown in the foyer of the British Library. The section of this letter shows an image that has been consciously designed using text only. There is a wide cultural history of creating pictures out of text, such as Taoist magic calligraphy, the recently developed ascii art (images generated from digital text) and Jewish micro-calligraphy. Micro-calligraphy is an art form that involves paintings constructed of texts made of Hebrew letters. In Safed, a small town in the north of Israel where Cabbalism was born, I saw galleries full of contemporary paintings that contained the entire text of the title, for example, a painting called 'Exodus' was made up of the Hebrew text for the Biblical story of Exodus. The meaning within the textual image is sometimes immediately obvious, as in this example. At other times it requires extra research and effort on the part of the reader who needs to explore beyond the text to make sense of it.

R. L.

Add.42502

Simonides Papers. Detail of letter from Simonides to John E. Hodgkin. Greek, 1860–1865. (VOL. I, F.388, p.22)

[illus. opposite]

Collision of ideas, reflections, echoes.
A human figure as the source of communication.
Dynamics of the written word.
Energy and movement deriving from writing.

My favourite colour is blue that's why I chose this one.
I am a writer from Tibet.
My language looks a lot like Sanskrit.

Anonymous public responses

Detail of astrono-
mical calendar in
pictorial form with
three concentric
revolving disks for
finding place of the
sun and the moon,
1420. (F.27)

———

[illus. previous page]

This tiny red leather book truly is an object of beauty, filled with an astounding variety of material. Small enough to fit in the palm of your hand it contains coloured sketches of saints, signs of the zodiac, details of eclipses, information about battles in Shrewsbury, Agincourt and Tewkesbury, and references to the martyrdom of St Thomas of Canterbury and the murder of Edward II. The latitude of ten towns is listed and in the fly leaves, in 15th-century hand, are meteorological notes forecasting the weather. There are a number of fascinating diagrams in the book including one that estimates the distance of the planets according to Rabbi Moyses, with notes on Arabic numerals, and another that details the division of the world between Shem, Ham and Japheth. Near the centre of this magical book is an almost three-dimensional diagram, made out of three concentric revolving vellum disks, designed to assist in finding the position of the sun and the moon. The disks are covered in red and brown ink in Latin script, including numbers and small sketches of moons and planets. It is still possible to gently turn these disks, which are fixed in the centre by a piece of leather string. The string has worn a small hole in the centre of the page, which hints at the age of the document. This is possibly the most mystical object I have called up, with references to science, religion, history and mythology. I photograph the central section and the image becomes the one most commonly talked about throughout the duration of this project. R.L.

This image conveys a wonderful forgotten sense of mystery and magic. An underlying tone seems to be asking questions about traditions and faith. The detail of the hand drawn marks and the care and effort that has gone into the lettering and design add to a sense of dedication and love which seem to exist around this image. This calendar communicates to me a blurring of science and religion. Its message seems to project a sense of security in an age of uncertainty.

Jonathon Hyer Student

Magical image-like astrological fragment on the transition from the Middle Ages into the age of scientific discovery, modernism and the machine world overlay the archetypal/planetary world of dream symbols.

John Pickering Professor of Psychology, Warwick University

There are round shapes and triangles. Oh, the shapes are things you can see in the sky. There's a fingernail moon, a whole moon, and a SUN!

Megan Age three years

Detail of astronomical calendar in pictorial form with three concentric revolving disks for finding place of the sun and the moon, 1420. (F.27)

———

[illus. page 69]

WD.4493

I look at each image as a series of marks waiting to be decoded.

When I visited the East India Office for the first time it was during the middle of researching a children's novel set partly in Bangladesh. I was searching for images of rural village life so I tried tapping the keyword 'Bangladesh' into the catalogue's search system and surprisingly got only one hit, WD.4493, Mike Massingham's artist's notebook. The book records a trip by the artist to India in 1986 and the pages are filled with graphic pen-and-ink and pencil sketches recording his journey. The drawings cover the usual street scenes, characters and events you would expect to see in any contemporary traveller's photo album, but there are also a few disturbing images of beggars with their eyelids stitched together and children dying on the streets. Much of the older material I have viewed in the Reading Rooms appears cruel or vulgar when read hundreds of years after it was written. It makes you wonder how those in the future will see these 20th-century drawings.

It is a detail from one of the more celebratory images that I decide to photograph: a sketch of dancers at a wedding party. I focus on a small section of people in motion, a collection of downward pencil marks. When viewed in isolation this image looks like fragments of a strange script – a picture waiting to be read. R.L.

Mike Massingham's sketchbook from India, 1986. (p. 102)

——

[illus. page 72]

Mike Massingham's sketchbook from India, 1986. (p. 102)

——

[illus. page 72]

As someone who works on the relationship between England and India in the c17th –c18th but has never been to India, I like the chaotic confusion and unknowability of this. It is impossible to tell what it is of. It could be letters or part of a drawing as the title suggests but I find it rather beautiful at the level of sheer pattern.

The image is a maelstrom of line and curvature. In it you see the depths of human life, the curved lines that are the wandering pathways of our lives. It also looks like a whirligig of a dance, where in the spinning and the complications there is a harmony, a purpose and a resolution.

This image blurs the boundary between handwriting and draughtsmanship. Loose letter-like forms are allowed to spread over the page with no regard for the systematic order in the normal demand from text. The impression of the swift execution, implied by the lines and the overlapping figures, calls to mind some forms of illustration, such as Quentin Blake's work. It also reminds me of Cy Twombly's paintings, which sometimes juxtapose words and images in an apparently disordered, haphazard manner. Eyes, spectacles and musical notes leap out from the jumble of figures.

Anonymous public responses

Squiggles are interesting. They remind me of my own handwriting and look like nonsense.

Lorcan Age 9 years

Royal 14.C.I

Historical works of
William Rishanger,
Martinus Polonus &
Geoffrey Monmouth.
Silhouette of dragon
in margins.
Latin, 14th century.
(Verso p.45)

———

[illus. previous page]

There is an atmosphere in the Manuscripts Reading Room of determined intensity which I find comforting. It is a room full of serious scholars who treat their chosen documents with the greatest respect. On this occasion I decide to take a second look at the manuscript containing the blank pages and the monks' fingerprints. As I turn the pages particles of ancient dust blow off them; I can taste them in my throat, acrid and bitter. It is the numerous gargoylish figures in the margins of the vellum pages that interest me this time – they look surprisingly contemporary.

On the reverse of page 45, a silhouette of a dragon can be clearly seen from the painting on the other side. Viewed close up through a magnifying glass you can see the animal hairs embedded into the surface of the vellum and the animal smell of the book increases the illusion that you are looking at a tattoo on skin, which is essentially what this image is. Isolated from its 14th-century context this medieval image takes on contemporary undertones. **R.L.**

Of all the images, this is for me the most intriguing. It brings to mind a golden monkey with arms outstretched. A picture of an endangered species often believed to be the embodiment of wise beings, Buddha-like, white and pale with golden soft fur. The form, the graceful pose, reminds me of monkeys in classical Chinese paintings. Of course this is my instant reaction, as upon closer inspection it looks like something completely different but the essence remains there for me, a mysterious monkey. The code 'Royal' adds to the impression, rare, royal, golden-yellow furry monkey-like creatures, beautiful.

Ming Wong Artist, Pearson Creative Research Fellow 2004, British Library

Historical works of William Rishanger, Martinus Polonus & Geoffrey Monmouth. Silhouette of dragon in margins.
Latin, 14th century.
(Verso p. 45)

[illus. page 75]

بدسته یکی سپرد بعد از رفقه آنرا وزیر ک...

روز دوم و سوم همینه دستور عمل کرد ...

مبلغ آنچه بغلام داده بود مقصود بنو...

مابقی آنرا غلامش بتمام ادا کرد همانکه ...

خاطرش فدح است و برادای آنچه گفتم ...

یواش شد و مبلغ نیز ب وقوف ... درعقب ...

خانه وبر بافتح جوه شب درآمد پر خواستم ...

نفیس بباراستم و بوبهای خوش معطر گردانید ...

رسانیدم و بکوفتم بکناد و بیرون آمد ...

شد و انالله و انا الیه راجعون گفت ...

I spent a considerable amount of time looking through a number of Hékékyan's journals. They are just such beautiful objects. The style and quality of the author's handiwork is exquisite, particularly, in my opinion, his Arabic script. Sadly, recent world news events have changed the potential meaning of a page of unknown Arabic writing.

I tried to get this particular page translated but the task proved nearly impossible as bookworms have literally eaten away so much of the text that its meaning can no longer be recovered. The intervention of paper conservators to stop the process of time and decay destroying this page completely can be felt more than visibly seen. Covering the surface of the page is a film of mesh-like fabric finer than a butterfly's wing that is literally holding the fragments of the page together. Seeing the skill involved in the repair of this book inspired me to visit the Conservation Department of the British Library where I spent an incredible day taking photographs of and talking to conservators at work. They showed me frail leaves of manuscripts that had been carefully washed and were drying on beds of hand-made papers. I saw a broken wooden binding painstakingly repaired with brass pins, and a tiny, ancient Somalian prayer book worn by monks in a minute, heavily stitched leather satchel. The satchel proved too fragile to be repaired and the conservator who showed it to me had spent weeks constructing a handmade box for it to rest in, filled with soft padded cushions.

R. L.

Add.37448

Autobiography written on a voyage to Egypt by Joseph Hékékyan Bey, an Egyptian in the Armenian service, 1830. (VOL.I, p.436)

———

[illus. opposite]

figure against the ... of the
conservationist. Particularly
binding ... fine thread
holes made by tiny paper
eating worms.

As soon as I see this image I can tell it is what we call an oriental text, not just because of the Arabic writing but because of the paper it's on and its fragile state. Paper from that part of the world and time period tends to be of a lower quality than western paper of the same period and due to the extremely hot and dry conditions of its environment (this one is from Egypt) it tends to deteriorate quickly. The netting over the paper has been put there probably in the fifties or sixties to literally hold the fragile material together. It used to be a last resort for material this fragile. We don't use this kind of method of conservation nowadays. In the past onion skins and chicken skins have been used for this purpose but nowadays we tend to use a very thin fibre tissue called spider tissue which is much subtler and can barely be seen or felt.

The worm holes on the page are interesting as they are part of a characteristic of this type of book. As conservators we like to fill all the holes but we don't anymore, we see it as part of the history of the book.

Mark Browne Conservation Department, The British Library

Add.37448

Autobiography written on a voyage to Egypt by Joseph Hékékyan Bey, an Egyptian in the Armenian service, 1830. (VOL. I, p.436)

[illus. page 78]

Pidgin-English

The light comes on my desk and I go to collect my latest requested item; a notebook belonging to C. G. Leland compiled in the 1870s. It is filled with different notes and letters, newspaper articles and lists that refer to the collection of words from a variety of languages. Leland seems to have roamed Europe without the back-up of audio recording equipment and documented his findings in this journal. There are pages full of translations, mainly of single everyday words. A large section of the book is taken up with a handwritten dictionary from Romany to English and there's another part that translates circus slang. A few pages make references to 'Schmussen, or the Jewish-German dialect', which I presume means Yiddish and there is a considerable amount of material on 'Pidgin-English', with illustrative notes from newspapers and oral sources, including the words of songs. It's a fascinating read and a beautiful thing in its own right. The pages look as though they have been gathered together over a long period of time and are obviously from different places and countries. This collection of material again makes me think about the beauty of the written word. Of course, if this research were conducted today the equipment used would be able to accurately capture the look and sound of these different people, making this research material more accessible to a wider audience, but something of the magic of this book would be lost through the process of digitisation. I have tried to describe what I mean by taking this photograph of the author's handwriting, which has been pasted onto a beautiful piece of coral paper. R.L.

Add.39561

C. G. Leland Collection 'Pidgin-English' with notes from newspapers and oral sources, 1875. (VOL. X, F.47)

———

[illus. opposite]

C. G. Leland
Collection 'Pidgin-
English' with notes
from newspapers
and oral sources,
1875. (VOL. X, F. 47)
———

[illus. page 82]

Denotatively this is a square coloured in a shade of pale orange. Within it there is an irregular rectangle. This is a coral colour. Within the rectangle there are two signs composed of the signifiers PIDGIN ENGLISH. Between these there is a small horizontal mark -.

Connotatively I can see what looks like a raggedy strip of sellotape stuck to perhaps, an old envelope. On the tape someone has written with a fountain pen, the words 'Pidgin English'. The elegance of the hand, the round loopy characters, the antique colour of the ink, the pale blush of peach, and of course the words themselves, evoke an unexpected associative memory: Me, 1991, Trafalgar Square, birds, sunset. I am waiting for a date (Australian) to arrive. As I idle by the lion closest to St Martin's, I am approached by a stranger, possibly male, possibly Spanish, asking for directions in broken English. I am pleased that I can direct him/her and do so as date arrives. This leaves me feeling useful, confident and like a native Londoner (which I am not). Pleasant romantic date ensues.

But I'm not sure if this really happened as, having lost zillions of little grey cells through clubbing and childbirth, my memory now speaks to me itself in Pidgin English. Spluttering half sentences, wafting puffs of atmosphere, it conveys only the essence of people and places from the past, leaving the current 'Me' to connotatively fill in the blanks. Sometimes I worry about this loss and decay, but generally, as a storyteller, I like it better this way.

Syd Moore Lecturer in Publishing, Essex University

ܘܡܫܟܐ

ܗܘ ܦܩ ܀

ܐܟܪܘܠܐ

ܐܟܪܒܘ ܗ ܠܥܠ ܀

Fragment of a letter
to Charles Kent
concerning a trans-
lation into Syriac,
October 27, 1879.

———

[illus. previous page]

Charles Kent was a contemporary and friend of Charles Dickens. He is best known for his work, the *Corona Catholica* (published in 1880). This consists of translations in over fifty different languages of an epigram about Leo XIII becoming Pope. Add.43457 is a collection of letters to Charles Kent that predate the publication of *Corona Catholica*, a sort of work in progress. As a writer I find it fascinating to see material that gives an insight into others' research processes when constructing a book for publication.

This folio consists mainly of correspondence from scholars who contributed to the project and the subject is their personal interpretations and translations of the epigram. They are written in Gaelic, Swedish, German, Danish, Icelandic and Hebrew, being just some of the languages I could recognise. They have been received from a professor of Arabic in Dublin, a Jesuit rector from Glasgow and a professor of Assyriology from Oxford University to name a few.

Near the back of the book is a letter from a Mr Strassmaier, an expert in ancient Syriac. He tells Kent it has been hard to give a literal translation to the epigram. His writing in English is almost as hard for me to decipher as the Syriac as I am not used to reading 19th-century handwriting. I find the Syriac text incredibly striking and photograph a small section of the translation. R. L.

Seeing words magnified and in different hues, it's so exciting… it seems like an archaeology of words and letters.

Anonymous public response

Islamic? Semitic? Fine horizontal lines added in electronic reprographic process add something even though they detract from what Walter Benjamin calls the "aura" of the fragment.

John Pickering Professor of Psychology, Warwick University

Add.43457

Fragment of a letter to Charles Kent concerning a translation into Syriac, October 27, 1879.

——

[illus. page 85]

Enter *Sentius, Lucius*

Lu[...]

[...]tion you have be ho[...]
[...] will transend my p[...]
[...] see such dayds as t[...]
[...] his Siege and retur[...]
[...]nes, although they have
[...]uyd by the overall Battdll[...]
[...] foile, although my Soldiers di[...]
[...] fortune against them, but now I [...]
and that from this time forward [...]
w[ch] is to maintaine this little pitta[...]
it will can regaine what doth [...]

You can only really start to appreciate the range of handwritten material in the Library by spending a considerable amount of time in the Reading Rooms looking at it. In one afternoon you can have works from ten different centuries in your hands. You can move from collections of letters, to medieval manuscripts, to 4th-century fragments of papyrus to the writings of a schoolboy from fifty years ago. My pleasure at examining these unique manuscripts grew as I became aware of the mass of material stored down in the basement. I began to imagine my chosen items being carefully removed from miles and miles of shelves deep underground and travelling up specially designed conveyor belts from the basement to the very top of the building.

This literary notebook did not disappoint. One of seven volumes, it is described in the catalogue as 'slightly imperfect'. The first page of the volume has been badly damaged by mould and mildew. This deterioration, the marks of time evident on the page, is what attracts me specifically to this manuscript. Examined under a magnifying glass the mould begins to take on its own landscape, looking like a rocky outcrop of an island coastline. Nearly half of the text is missing, appearing buried like an ancient mosaic at an archaeological site waiting to be excavated. The decay has been stopped in its tracks by the skill of conservators who have managed to preserve the remainder of the document, which is dotted throughout with tiny repairs. R.L.

Castle Ashby manuscripts. Handwritten text and mildew, 17th century. (VOL. VII, p. 1)

[illus. opposite]

Castle Ashby
manuscripts.
Handwritten
text and mildew,
17th century.
(VOL. VII, p. 1)

———

[illus. page 88]

I can instantly see this is a western manuscript. The paper is probably made from cotton rags, meaning it's good quality, and will usually last a long time. At some point in its history this page must have got wet and that's how the mould has developed. It is one letter from a collection of letters and it is our job as conservators to bind them together as a book to keep for future reference. I like working on correspondence best, thinking about all the different places the letters have come from. They may have been kept in a box or under a bed or travelled from place to place, coming together as a collection years after they were originally written. Letters often experience a more varied amount of environments and atmospheric conditions than books, making them, in my opinion, more interesting to work on.

This letter has been conserved in different ways. In the corner there is a clearly visible paper repair. The mould on the page has also been stopped in its tracks by conservators at some point. This is quite a simple process involving drying the paper completely and brushing away the spores of mould. If this page ever became moist again the mould could come back to life and charge across the page, destroying everything in sight and anything else it came into contact with.

The mould on this page is a trait of where it has been stored. I imagine there could be a great story behind how it got wet in the first place.

Mark Browne Conservation Department, The British Library

gily knight "
rold sit Row

YOU ARE NOT TRYNG

ong, long ago
he old story tell
ay There lived in B
a great king na
their whoes Pala
d Court were at

Add. 70828

Part of my fellowship was spent running workshops called *Meet a Writer*, mainly for primary school groups. I revealed my own research methods to the children and took them to the John Ritblat Gallery of Treasures to look at famous writers' work in progress. We spent time looking at Beatles memorabilia, in particular a song written in felt pen on the back of a children's book where the text is full of crossings out. My favourite artefact in the Gallery is a journal belonging to James Joyce. The open pages reveal a chaotic mess of illegible pencil markings, which thrilled the children when they learnt the fame of the author of this messy page.

In the Reading Rooms I came across many such examples of writer's work in progress including some unpublished works from early periods in the writer's lives, such as a school exercise book belonging to Auberon Waugh, the son of Evelyn Waugh.

Auberon never achieved the fame of his father but he did become a well-known and respected journalist, political satirist and columnist for the Daily Telegraph. His schoolbook is filled with sloppy handwriting in pencil and littered with irate comments from his English teacher. In bright red pencil the teacher has dotted remarks throughout the book including the one I have chosen to photograph, 'YOU ARE NOT TRY[I]NG,' ironically misspelled by the teacher. I'm sure the young Auberon would have found this immensely funny.

How much can one childhood schoolbook reveal about the person you grow up to be? When looking at tributes left to Auberon after his death I found this one on the BBC News web-site from Duncan Fine of Australia;

'I don't think he wrote what he felt so much as he wrote what he knew would annoy the greatest number of people for the greatest length of time'. R.L.

Auberon Waugh had achieved such a unique status in British literary life that his death in 2001 prompted a positive outpouring of grief, even amongst those he frequently ridiculed. The obituaries went to extremes, of course. Auberon would certainly have been amused to find himself described as the 'pole position polemicist' or 'flaneur/curmudgeon'. Indeed, those brave enough to criticise the editor of the Literary Review and candidate for the Dog Lovers' Party endured more than a frisson of hostility. Nevertheless, the chief criticism leveled at Waugh was that his continuous abuse and distrust of most politicians was nothing more than an 'idle unwillingness to engage with any politician's attempt to make life better...'. However, regardless of the adoration, admonishments or attempts at indifference, there was nothing indifferent about Waugh's genius for satire.

I love this image from Master Waugh's exercise book. I imagine his early refusal to find anything admirable about rote descriptions of English history, and yet, amazingly, here it is already, that accusation of idleness. Better still is his opponent's certainly deliberate misspelling of 'trying' as 'tryng'. In this brilliant exchange I imagine the schooling of a satirist. Young Auberon has already learnt to demonstrate disregard for mediocre material, and is being shown by his teacher how to ridicule one's opponents through mimicry. Waugh went on to conquer the twin peaks of insult and injury saying, 'Looking back... at all the people I have insulted, I am mildly surprised that I am allowed to exist', but surely one of his crowning achievements must be the mock-lazy title of his autobiography, *Will this do?*, calculated as it was to further enrage his critics. A classic example of a technique learnt years before in the school for satire.

Mark Diaper Berlin, Germany

Detail from Auberon Waugh's school exercise book, 1947.

[illus. page 91]

Rachel Lichtenstein is the British Library's first Pearson Creative Research Fellow. An artist and writer whose recent projects include a book with Artangel, curating an exhibition at The Women's Library entitled *Keeping Pace: Older Women of the East End* and a multi-media installation at The Whitechapel Gallery's Centenary Show. Rachel's first book *Rodinsky's Room* (Granta 1999) has been published in five languages. She is currently working on three new books for Hamish & Hamilton.

The aims of The Pearson Creative Research Fellowship are:

- To provide groups of learners with an encounter with a professional creative person making use of the collection. These encounters include language and arts workshops and sharing creative research, interpretations of collection items and discussion with learners on the website www.bl.uk/learning

- To provide a high-profile individual face to the British Library Learning's strategic emphasis on 'research skills' – to show that these skills are not about data retrieval but about solving problems, making personal meaning from discovered sources, debating meanings with others and communicating ideas.

- To expose the richness of the British Library: to show that it holds not just books but much more, from a world of cultures.

- To approach the Library's collection displays and digital databases as 'a museum of thought' and to help us form an engaging critical framework for a deeper exploration of our collections.

- To generate creative products such as writing or art work, showing that these are not created in isolation and that library research is open to all.

The second Pearson Creative Research Fellow is the video artist Ming Wong.

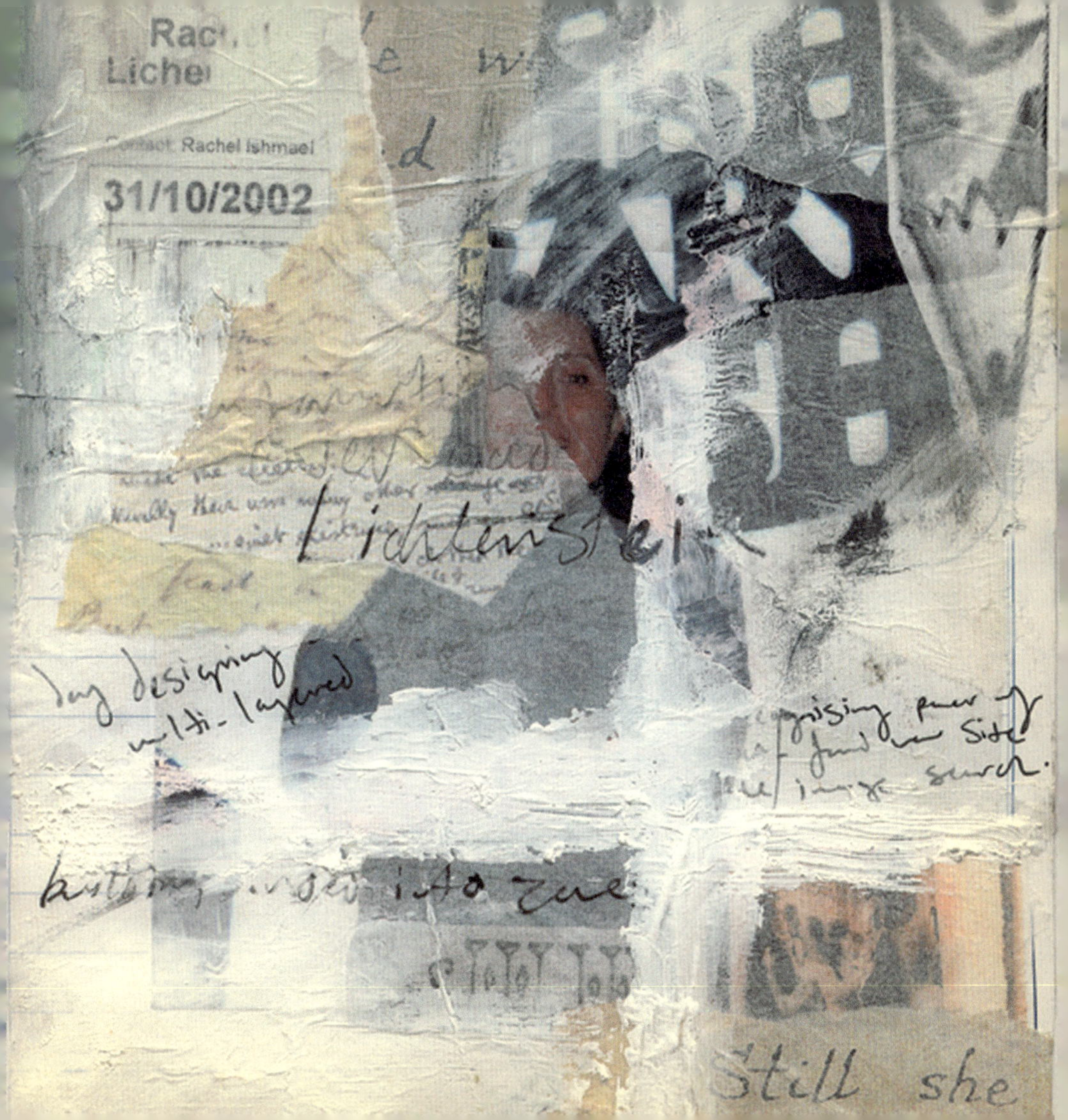
Rachel Ishmael
31/10/2002
Lichtenstein
Still she

Acknowledgements

Firstly I would like to thank Pearson for funding my fellowship. Many thanks to Bridget McKenzie, Head of Learning, for her vision in creating the fellowship and for her support and encouragement. Thanks to the rest of the education team, including Tim Saward, Sophie Weeks, Ria Bartlett, Cecilia Ishmael and Livvy Adjei. A big thank you to Laurence Pordes from the Photography Department for creating such beautiful images and to the librarians and staff of the various Reading Rooms for their help. Thanks to Mark Browne, Vicki Humphreys and everyone in the Conservation Department who allowed me to photograph them at work. Thanks to Rob Perks of the British Library Sound Archive for his support and a particular thanks to Chris Fletcher, Curator of Manuscripts, and to Jennifer Howes of the India Office Archives. Many thanks to Geraldine Kenny and the Exhibitions team for all their hard work, to Lara Speicher in Publishing and to Mark Diaper who designed this book. And a very special thanks to everyone who contributed to this publication with their responses to the images. **Rachel Lichtenstein**